ARE THESE
the
LAST DAYS?

The Crucial Questions Series
By R.C. Sproul

CRUCIAL
QUESTIONS
No. | 20

ARE THESE
the
LAST DAYS?

R.C. SPROUL

ℝ *Reformation Trust*   A DIVISION OF LIGONIER MINISTRIES, ORLANDO, FL

Are These the Last Days?

© 2014 by R.C. Sproul

Published by Reformation Trust Publishing
A division of Ligonier Ministries
421 Ligonier Court, Sanford, FL 32771
Ligonier.org   ReformationTrust.com

Printed in North Mankato, MN
Corporate Graphics
October 2015
First edition, second printing

Cover design: Gearbox Studios
Interior design and typeset: Katherine Lloyd, The DESK

All Scripture quotations are from *The Holy Bible, English Standard Version*, copyright © 2001 by Crossway Bibles, a division of Good News Publishers. Used by permission. All rights reserved.

Library of Congress Cataloging-in-Publication Data

Sproul, R. C. (Robert Charles), 1939-
  Are these the last days? / by R.C. Sproul. -- First edition.
    pages cm. -- (Crucial questions series ; No. 20)
  ISBN 978-1-56769-376-8 -- ISBN 1-56769-376-8
1. Bible. Matthew XXIV--Criticism, interpretation, etc. 2. Jesus Christ--Prophecies. 3. Second Advent--Biblical teaching. I. Title.
  BS2575.52.S68 2014
  236'.9--dc23

                                                2014006859

Contents

THE DESTRUCTION
OF THE TEMPLE

In the middle of the nineteenth century, a serious potato famine struck the nation of Ireland. Facing starvation, multitudes of people fled to other countries to seek sustenance. Some boarded ships and sailed for the New World, with many finally landing in New York City. Among those immigrants was my great-grandfather, who came to the United States from Donegal in the northern province of Ulster. Since he wanted his children and grandchildren to remember their heritage, he told tales of former days in Ireland and encouraged all of the family to learn the songs of the Irish people. My mother sang Irish lullabies to us and permitted my sister and me to stay home from school each year on Saint Patrick's Day, when the Pittsburgh radio stations played Irish songs all day.

However, to this day, I think of myself more as an American than an Irishman. Although I've been to Europe many times, I've yet to go back to Ireland. On the other hand, my son has been more zealous about our ancestry, making sure that all eight of his children have Irish names. And as a tribute to his ancestry, he wore a kilt to his ordination service.

At my house, we left many of the markers of our ethnic identity behind, but for a Jew in antiquity, this would certainly not have been the case. The Jews are one of the most remarkable groups of people who have ever populated the face of the earth. In the first century AD alone, their nation was conquered, their temple destroyed, and their capital, Jerusalem, was burned to the ground, killing an estimated 1.1 million Jews. After this, most Jews were dispersed to the four corners of the world. They went to what are the modern-day nations of Russia, Poland, Hungary, Germany, and Holland, and to many other places.

Even though Jews have been without a homeland for most of the past two millennia, they have never lost their ethnic and national identity.

This remarkable phenomenon is predicted in detail in the Olivet Discourse.

One of the most important and controversial chapters in all of the New Testament, the discourse, which is found in Matthew 24, is one of the most dramatic prophecies given by our Lord.

> Jesus left the temple and was going away, when his disciples came to point out to him the buildings of the temple. But he answered them, "You see all these, do you not? Truly, I say to you, there will not be left here one stone upon another that will not be thrown down."
>
> As he sat on the Mount of Olives, the disciples came to him privately, saying, "Tell us, when will these things be, and what will be the sign of your coming and of the end of the age?" . . .
>
> "From the fig tree learn its lesson: as soon as its branch becomes tender and puts out its leaves, you know that summer is near. So also, when you

see all these things, you know that he is near, at the very gates. Truly, I say to you, this generation will not pass away until all these things take place. Heaven and earth will pass away, but my words will not pass away." (Matt. 24:1–3, 32–35)

Before we consider this text, I'd like you to consider a "what if" scenario. Suppose I were to claim that last night I received a special revelation from God. I declare that I now have the gift of prophecy and will give you a prediction of things that are to come to pass. I predict that sometime within the next twelve months, the United States will fall, the Capitol building in Washington will be destroyed, the White House will be demolished, the fifty states of the union will be dissolved, and the United States as an independent nation will cease to exist. Finally, I don't know the exact timing, but only that it will happen sometime within the next twelve months.

Without question, within the next twelve months, you would know for certain whether my claim was true or false. If it didn't come to pass, you would be justified in labeling me a false prophet, unworthy of your attention.

I give this illustration to demonstrate what is at stake in

the text. In all of the Bible, I cannot think of any prophecy more astonishing than the prophecy that our Lord Jesus gave on the Mount of Olives concerning the temple and Jerusalem. In Luke's account, He told the disciples that not one stone of the Herodian temple would be left on top of one another and that the city of Jerusalem itself would be destroyed (Luke 21:6, 24). This was a truly shocking claim. Herod's temple was magnificent, to say the least. The temple's stones were as large as sixteen feet long and eight feet high. In the first century, if there was any building that seemed impregnable, it was the temple in Jerusalem. When Jesus made this prediction, the Jewish people would have considered Him either a lunatic or a prophet endowed with supernatural knowledge.

Of course, we know that Jesus had supreme authority to make these claims, and history has vindicated Him. These things came to pass in perfect detail; as foretold by Jesus, the temple was destroyed in AD 70 and the Jews were dispersed throughout the world. This prophecy about the destruction of Jerusalem and the temple provides firm proof of the identity of Jesus and the inspiration of Scripture by the Holy Spirit, and it should close the mouth of even the most hardened skeptic.

After Jesus made this astonishing prediction, the disciples immediately came to Him and wanted to know the exact timing of His predictions. Jesus then engaged in a long discussion of the signs of the times, and gave a description of the great tribulation and of His return.

In recent days, these topics have seen increased interest. Books such as Hal Lindsey's *The Late, Great Planet Earth* and the *Left Behind* series have been wildly popular. Everyone is interested in the timing and exact details of Jesus' return. However, Jesus' answer to the question of timing creates some challenges for us. He says in verse 34, "Truly, I say to you, this generation will not pass away until all these things take place."

Do you see the problem? To the Jews, the term *generation* referred to a time frame of roughly forty years. So, Jesus seemed to be saying that the destruction of temple, the destruction of Jerusalem, and His appearance at the end of the age were all going to take place within forty years. Many critics thus reject Jesus because they believe He was saying that His return, the end of the world, and the consummation of His kingdom would all take place within four decades.

How do we deal with this? The critics deal with it very

simply. They say Jesus was partially right in His predictions and partially wrong. Therefore, He was a false prophet. Others say He was completely right in His prediction and that every New Testament prophecy (i.e., His return, the future resurrection, the rapture of the saints, etc.) was fulfilled in the first century, leaving nothing for future fulfillment. I don't agree with either of these positions.

I am convinced that what Jesus is talking about in this passage had special reference to a judgment of Christ coming on the Jewish nation, thus ending the age of the Jews. This Jewish age ended with the destruction of Jerusalem and the dispersion of the Jews, which triggered the beginning of the New Testament time period, which is later called "the age of the Gentiles." This is where we still find ourselves today.

In the next few chapters, I'm going to interpret the Olivet Discourse in a manner that I believe is consistent with the way that it would have been understood by the disciples at that time. When Jesus is asked when these things will happen, He says, "I can't tell you the day and the hour, but I can tell you with absolute certainty that this generation will not pass away until all of these things take place." I believe our Lord was speaking the unvarnished truth.

THE SIGNS
OF THE TIMES

In the previous chapter, I mentioned the difficulties that accompany Jesus' prediction of the destruction of Jerusalem and the temple. Jesus made the bold statement that the generation of His hearers would not pass away until "the end." As we saw in the last chapter, this creates many interpretive challenges, especially in reference to Jesus' final return. How are we to understand His words concerning His coming, the end times, and the gospel being preached to all the nations? Was Jesus mistaken in His time frame? How do we reconcile this account? Let's begin by taking a closer look at verses 3–14 of Matthew 24.

As he sat on the Mount of Olives, the disciples came to him privately, saying, "Tell us, when will these things be, and what will be the sign of your coming and of the end of the age?" And Jesus answered them, "See that no one leads you astray. For many will come in my name, saying, 'I am the Christ,' and they will lead many astray. And you will hear of wars and rumors of wars. See that you are not alarmed, for this must take place, but the end is not yet. For nation will rise against nation, and kingdom against kingdom, and there will be famines and earthquakes in various places. All these are but the beginning of the birth pains.

"Then they will deliver you up to tribulation and put you to death, and you will be hated by all nations for my name's sake. And then many will fall away and betray one another and hate one another. And many false prophets will arise and lead many astray. And because lawlessness will be increased, the love of many will grow cold. But the one who endures to the end will be saved. And this gospel of the kingdom will be proclaimed throughout the whole world as a testimony to all nations, and then the end will come." (Matt. 24:3–14)

As I suggest possible ways to understand this text, we have to tread very carefully and with a fair amount of humility. While I've wrestled with this passage for many years, I do not propose an infallible interpretation. Though I am convinced that there is merit to my conclusions, I am aware that many Christians throughout history have debated this subject and have come to different conclusions. I simply lend my voice to the discussion.

Historically, as I have already mentioned in the previous chapter, there have been numerous ways to interpret Jesus' words in Matthew 24. Some critics say Jesus was simply wrong and thus deem Him a false prophet. Others have tried to interpret the term *generation* to mean something other than a time frame of about forty years. Still others have made the case that Jesus was only speaking about the immediate future and not His second coming and the end of history as we know it. Others have pointed to a two-fold approach to fulfillment, a primary fulfillment in the first century and an ultimate fulfillment at the end of history. This is often the case with prophecies from the Old Testament.

Verse 3 reads, "Tell us, when will these things be, and what will be the sign of your coming and of the end of the age?" (v. 3b). We should exercise caution when considering the disciples' question. What did they mean by "age"? Customarily, many say that "the end of the age" refers to Jesus' return to consummate His kingdom here on earth. But could there be any other possible interpretations? Typically, when we say "end of an age," we are referring to a particular era defined by certain characteristics, such as the Iron Age, the Bronze Age, or the Ice Age. Many believe this passage is making a distinction between the age of the Jews and the age of the Gentiles.

To explore the meaning of "the end of the age," let's consider Luke's account of the Olivet Discourse, which gives us further information:

> But when you see Jerusalem surrounded by armies,
> then know that its desolation has come near. Then

let those who are in Judea flee to the mountains, and let those who are inside the city depart, and let not those who are out in the country enter it, for these are days of vengeance, to fulfill all that is written. Alas for women who are pregnant and for those who are nursing infants in those days! For there will be great distress upon the earth and wrath against this people. They will fall by the edge of the sword and be led captive among all nations, and Jerusalem will be trampled underfoot by the Gentiles, until the times of the Gentiles are fulfilled. (Luke 21:20–24)

Jesus is giving a warning to His followers, telling them what to do when they see the armies surrounding Jerusalem. The advice He gives is completely counterintuitive to any usual response to an invading army or military siege. In the ancient world, in the case of an invasion, people would leave their homes and possessions and flee for refuge in a walled city. This is the very reason there were walls around cities in the ancient world. They were built as a defense against invaders.

When Jesus spoke these words, the walls of Jerusalem

were one hundred and fifty feet high. When the Romans attacked Jerusalem in AD 70, they had to besiege the city, and even with their military might, they found it a Herculean task to get through those walls. The siege lasted many months, so long that by the end of the struggle, the Mount of Olives was completely bare of olive trees; Roman soldiers encamped on the mount had cut all the trees down and burned them for warmth.

But Jesus said, "When you see the armies coming, don't go to the city. Go to the mountains. Go to the desert. Go anywhere but Jerusalem, because in Jerusalem you will not find safety, but only destruction."

When Jerusalem fell and the city was destroyed, more than a million Jews were killed. But the Christians followed Jesus' advice and fled beyond the city. Luke's account says, "these are days of vengeance," meaning God's wrath was poured out upon His people. When Jesus wept over Jerusalem, He was weeping for His people, who rejected Him and would suffer the punishment for this rejection.

We must not miss this portion of Luke 21: "They will fall by the edge of the sword and be led captive among all nations, and Jerusalem will be trampled underfoot by the Gentiles, until the times of the Gentiles are fulfilled"

(v. 24). All of this happened. Jesus makes a distinction between the times of the Gentiles and the times of the Jews. In the eleventh chapter of Romans, Paul deals with the question of ethnic Israel and whether God will work again with the Jewish people. He says that once the time of the Gentiles is fulfilled, there will be a new outreach to ethnic Israel.

I will never forget watching the news in 1967 as the Jews fought for the city of Jerusalem. When they got to the Wailing Wall, the Jewish soldiers threw their rifles down and ran to the last surviving temple wall and began to pray. I wept because what I was seeing was so amazing. Was this the fulfillment of Luke 21? Biblical scholars were reading the Bible in one hand and a newspaper in the other and asking, "Are we now near the end of the times of the Gentiles?"

In the Olivet Discourse, when Jesus spoke about "the end of the age," I am convinced that He wasn't talking about the end of the world, but about the end of the Jewish age. When Jerusalem fell, the age of the Jews, which spanned from Abraham to AD 70, ended. It marked the beginning of the times of the Gentiles.

However, Jesus gives a few caveats as He answers His

disciples' question of when these things will take place. He didn't want them to be deceived that the end had already come when it hadn't, so He gave them a list of what we call "signs of the times." These were signs that had to happen before the end would come. Most people believe Jesus was describing the signs that will come right before the final consummation of His kingdom. We then have a tendency to pay careful attention to current events, wondering if they show any evidence that we are in the end times. But if we look carefully at this passage, we learn that Jesus is not talking about the signs that trigger the end of time, but the signs that had to take place before the destruction of Jerusalem. Consider the passage more carefully:

> For many will come in my name, saying, "I am the Christ," and they will lead many astray. And you will hear of wars and rumors of wars. See that you are not alarmed, for this must take place, but the end is not yet. For nation will rise against nation, and kingdom against kingdom, and there will be famines and earthquakes in various places. All these are but the beginning of the birth pains. (Matt. 24:5–8)

Reflect upon these signs: people claiming to be the Christ, false prophets, wars and rumors of wars, famines, pestilences, and earthquakes. How can these things be signs? When are there not wars and rumors of wars? When are there not earthquakes? When are there not famines? There have also always been false prophets and false christs. If these things have always been with us, in what sense could they be signs?

In order for these things to be signs, they would have to happen in a significant way and in a significant time frame. This is the very meaning of the word *significant*: literally, "having sign-value." The problem is further complicated if we assume that Jesus is not talking about signs that the disciples themselves would observe, but signs that were going to happen two thousand years in the future.

The Jewish historian Josephus wrote much concerning these signs that Jesus mentioned. He wrote about the numerous false prophets among the Jews, many claiming to be the Messiah. He also reported four severe famines between AD 41 and 50 in which many people starved to death. He reports two very serious earthquakes, one during the reign of Caligula and the second during the reign of Claudius. Next came Nero, who ushered in a great persecution against Christians. Jesus alludes to this: "Then they will deliver you up to tribulation and put you to death, and you will be hated by all nations for my name's sake. And then many will fall away and betray one another and hate one another" (Matt. 24:9–10).

Jesus speaks of His followers being persecuted, being killed, and betraying one another. This took place under Caligula and Nero as well. The great fire that destroyed Rome was allegedly set by Nero himself. But in order to deflect guilt, he accused the Christians of setting the fire, which ignited a time of great persecution. He even used Christians as human torches to illumine gardens, and in his madness unleashed horrible persecution against the Jews, particularly those who were in Rome. He killed many of the Christians' leaders, including the Apostles Paul and Peter. Surely this fulfilled what Jesus told His disciples.

Jesus was proven right. Everything that He said would happen actually took place. And it happened in a significant way to the people to whom Jesus gave these warnings. He wasn't giving His first-century disciples a warning about what was going to happen in the twenty-first century. He was saying, "Watch out for what's happening between now and the time Jerusalem is destroyed." But, He had a lot more to say, including the warning of the appearance of "the abomination of desolation." We'll consider this teaching in the next chapter.

THE GREAT
TRIBULATION

In the year 168 BC, the pagan ruler Antiochus IV Epiphanes had the audacity to build a pagan altar in the Jewish temple. Instead of sacrificing bulls, goats, or lambs, he desecrated the temple by sacrificing a pig. This was the height of blasphemy, because the Jews viewed pigs as unclean. This foul desecration provoked one of the most important Jewish revolutions against foreign invaders.

We have to understand how important the holiness of

God was and is for the Jewish people. The Jews believed that the temple was sacred and holy because the Holy One of Israel made His dwelling there. To them, this was the most sacred place in the world. To defile it with pagan sacrifices was the greatest insult that you could inflict upon Israel.

Faithful Jews saw in this atrocity the fulfillment of a prophecy found in the book of Daniel that refers to the "abomination of desolation" or the "abomination that makes desolate" (Dan. 9:27; 11:31; 12:11). Jesus seizes upon this term as He continues in His Olivet Discourse:

> So when you see the abomination of desolation spoken of by the prophet Daniel, standing in the holy place (let the reader understand), then let those who are in Judea flee to the mountains. Let the one who is on the housetop not go down to take what is in his house, and let the one who is in the field not turn back to take his cloak. And alas for women who are pregnant and for those who are nursing infants in those days! Pray that your flight may not be in winter or on a Sabbath. For then there will be great tribulation, such as has not been from the beginning of the world until now,

no, and never will be. And if those days had not been cut short, no human being would be saved. But for the sake of the elect those days will be cut short. Then if anyone says to you, "Look, here is the Christ!" or "There he is!" do not believe it. For false christs and false prophets will arise and perform great signs and wonders, so as to lead astray, if possible, even the elect. See, I have told you beforehand. So, if they say to you, "Look, he is in the wilderness," do not go out. If they say, "Look, he is in the inner rooms," do not believe it. For as the lightning comes from the east and shines as far as the west, so will be the coming of the Son of Man. Wherever the corpse is, there the vultures will gather. (Matt. 24:15–28)

The reference to "the abomination of desolation" is mysterious, but it is critical; it is the supreme sign to indicate the nearness of the fulfillment of these prophecies. Antiochus' idolatry was certainly abominable, but this event took place in the past, and Jesus is referring to something that will take place in the future. But what did Jesus have in view?

In AD 40, Emperor Caligula of Rome commanded that a statue of himself be built and placed inside the temple. You can imagine how this provoked the people of Israel. By the goodness of God's providence, Caligula died before that profanation took place.

In AD 69, one year before the destruction of Jerusalem and of the temple, something unprecedented took place. A sect of radical Jews called Zealots forcefully took over the temple and made it into a type of military base. The Zealots were a group of Jews who were passionate about the violent overthrow of their Roman occupiers. Once they took over the temple, they committed all kinds of atrocities within it, paying no respect to the holiness of God. The historian Josephus expressed his passionate denunciation of the horrible desecration that the Zealots committed against the temple. Was this what Jesus had in mind?

One other possible interpretation could be the presence of the Roman standards themselves. When the Roman armies marched, they carried their banners with the Roman standards emblazoned upon them. The Jews considered these images to be idolatrous. The presence of these standards in the temple would also have been considered an abomination.

While it's difficult to be certain which particular incident Jesus had in view, what we do know is that during the siege of Jerusalem His people followed His instructions. Remember that Jesus said in verse 15, "Let those who are in Judea flee to the mountains." This charge from Jesus would have been completely counterintuitive for His audience. When an invading army came, the normal procedure in the ancient world have been to flee to the nearest impregnable walled city they could find. Of course, in Judea, that would have been Jerusalem. But Jesus told His disciples, "When all these events happen, don't go to Jerusalem. Go to the mountains. Run for the hills." This is exactly what happened in AD 70. We know that around one million Jews were killed, but the Christians had fled.

Jesus continues His instructions: "Let the one who is on the housetop not go down to take what is in his house, and let the one who is in the field not turn back to take his cloak. And alas for women who are pregnant and for those who are nursing infants in those days! Pray that your flight may not be in winter or on a Sabbath" (vv. 17–20). This is obviously a message of urgency. We know that the Jewish people had flat roofs on their houses with outside stairs that went up to them. They would use the roof as a type of patio, a place to relax in the evening as the weather cooled. Jesus is saying to them, "Don't waste any time. As soon as you're aware of the presence of the abomination of desolation, leave quickly. Don't pack any bags. If you are in the field, don't return home to get any extra clothes. Whatever you're wearing or whatever you have in your pack, take that and forget everything else."

The note of urgency sounds again in the following verses. Time was of the essence, and quite simply, it is hard to be quick and mobile when you are pregnant or nursing. Winter seasons are the most difficult for outdoor survival, and having these signs come to pass on the Sabbath would have been challenging for the Jew because of the prohibitions against traveling long distances. Jesus is telling His followers to pray that these things don't happen at the wrong time so that nothing will impede their escape.

He continues in verses 21 and 22, "For then there will be great tribulation, such as has not been from the beginning of the world until now, no, and never will be. And if those days had not been cut short, no human being would be saved. But for the sake of the elect those days will be cut short."

Josephus records the fact that political upheaval in

Rome indeed shortened the destructive siege, allowing for more survivors than normally would have been expected. Based on what we know of that time period, it seems clear that Jesus was talking about a near-future event for His original audience, not something centuries and centuries down the road.

Jesus then says in verses 23 and 24, "Then if anyone says to you, 'Look, here is the Christ!' or 'There he is!' do not believe it. For false christs and false prophets will arise and perform great signs and wonders, so as to lead astray, if possible, even the elect." There is a widely held view in the church that Satan is as powerful as God and is engaged in a duel of miracles with Him, performing miracles to support his lies. It is believed that these miracles could even deceive God's people. I don't believe for one second that Satan ever did or ever will have the ability to perform a bona fide miracle. The signs and wonders of the false christs and prophets are not authentic signs and wonders in the service of a lie. Rather, they're *false* signs and wonders. They're tricks designed to deceive.

We should be concerned about the view that Satan can perform authentic miracles taking hold in the church. In the New Testament, the Apostolic writers appeal to the miracles of Jesus and the Apostles as proof that they were the true agents of revelation. They were the visible proof that God was with them. But if Satan can do a miracle, then the New Testament view of miracles as a means to authenticate the gospel message becomes invalid. When a miracle takes place, how could you ever know if it was from God or from Satan? This doesn't mean that God's people can't be deceived by trickery. Clearly, we can, or else Jesus wouldn't have warned against it.

Jesus continues in verses 26–28, "So, if they say to you, 'Look, he is in the wilderness,' do not go out. If they say, 'Look, he is in the inner rooms,' do not believe it. For as the lightning comes from the east and shines as far as the west, so will be the coming of the Son of Man. Wherever the corpse is, there the vultures will gather." When Jesus appears, this moment of catastrophic judgment will be like lightning. Lightning flashes and instantly goes across the sky. You don't even have time to measure its duration.

How should we understand His last statement concerning corpses and vultures? One of the reasons predictive prophecy is so difficult to interpret is that symbolic imagery is challenging to understand. The safest way to interpret images in apocalyptic literature is to understand how those images are used throughout the whole Bible. This principle can help us, but doesn't always solve every difficulty. While we can't say with certainty what Jesus means by this last statement, some of the finest New Testament scholars have suggested one creative interpretation. Most people have seen how scavenger birds circle over an animal that has recently died. Interestingly, the chief symbol of the Roman army was an eagle. Perhaps Jesus is saying that Rome is like a bird of prey. God will be the agent of punishment upon His people, and right before His wrath is poured out, "the eagles" will be circling.

Chapter Four

THE COMING
OF THE SON OF MAN

It's been said that the whole history of philosophy is nothing more than a footnote to the theories of Plato and Aristotle. When Plato established his academy in the outskirts of Athens, he was driven by a single passion in his quest for truth. According to Plato, that passion was to "save the phenomena." What did he mean by that? He was looking for the objective truth that makes the study of science possible. We can only understand observable data (or phenomena) if we have a sure foundation to stand upon. Plato was looking for an ultimate theory that would give clarity to all the mysteries and puzzles of this world. He wanted to discover the ideas that would explain the data that come to us through our five senses.

The renowned theoretical physicist Stephen Hawking has announced that we don't need God to explain the creation. His way of saving the phenomena is to affirm what he calls "spontaneous generation." For him, this means that the universe created itself. But it is sheer nonsense to assert that something can create itself or can come into being by its own power.

What does all this have to do with the Olivet Discourse? Quite simply, in regard to the Olivet Discourse, I have been trying to save the phenomena. I am trying to construct a framework that will allow us to make sense of Jesus' words.

To that end, let's consider what Jesus says after explaining the signs that would come just before the destruction of Jerusalem and the temple—"immediately after the tribulation of those days" (v. 29). Our section for this chapter could be most difficult section of the Olivet Discourse. Jesus says:

Immediately after the tribulation of those days the sun will be darkened, and the moon will not give its light, and the stars will fall from heaven, and the powers of the heavens will be shaken. Then will appear in heaven the sign of the Son of Man, and then all the tribes of the earth will mourn, and they will see the Son of Man coming on the clouds of heaven with power and great glory. And he will send out his angels with a loud trumpet call, and they will gather his elect from the four winds, from one end of heaven to the other.

From the fig tree learn its lesson: as soon as its branch becomes tender and puts out its leaves, you know that summer is near. So also, when you see all these things, you know that he is near, at the very gates. Truly, I say to you, this generation will not pass away until all these things take place. Heaven and earth will pass away, but my words will not pass away. (Matt. 24:29–35)

Imagine being with Jesus right after hearing all that He said. It seems obvious that you'd want to ask, "When will these things take place?" He makes it clear that these things won't happen until other specific events take place. He then uses the word "immediately" to recount what will happen next. Not two thousand years later, but *immediately*.

Our interpretive task becomes even more difficult in the following verses. We know from the facts of history that all the things that Jesus predicted about the destruction of Jerusalem came to pass. But what about verse 29, which says, "The sun will be darkened, and the moon will not give its light, and the stars will fall from heaven"? You can imagine how the skeptics of the Bible would love to use this text. They could easily say, "O yes! The temple is gone. Jerusalem was destroyed. The Jews were dispersed throughout the world. But the sun is still shining, and the moon is still there at night, and this calamitous portrait of all of these astronomical perturbations that were going to accompany the coming of the Son of Man did not take place. Therefore, Christ's prediction failed to come to pass." It gets worse as we read what Jesus says in verses 33 and 34: "So also, when you see all these things, you know that he is near, at the very gates. Truly, I say to you, this generation will not pass away until all these things take place."

There are many scholars for whom I have the utmost respect who come to very strange conclusions when dealing with this text. They try every way imaginable to remove this portion of Jesus' prediction from the context in which we find it. But it seems clear that Jesus meant to discuss these things all as one unit. So, how should we understand this text?

There are various options. One is to invoke the principle of primary and secondary fulfillments of prophecy. When prophecies are made, they can have an initial fulfillment within a time frame of one generation and then have an ultimate fulfillment many years later. This is a true possibility. But even if that's the case, we're still left with the problem of explaining the description of the sun being blotted out and all the rest of these astronomical perturbations. There is no record of these things taking place.

Another approach is to consider the time frame. Phrases such as "this generation will not pass away" or words like "immediately" may be taken not literally, but figuratively. Many commentators prefer this approach. They believe the reference to "this generation" is a figurative reference to a certain *type* of person. It doesn't actually refer to a rough time frame of forty years. In addition, many would understand Jesus' references to His return to be figurative as well.

It seems that a key question that should be asked is, How

are time frame references usually described in the Bible? Are they usually described figuratively or literally? More practical still for this discussion, how are predictions of God's cosmic judgment usually described? Literally or figuratively?

There is a helpful pattern in Old Testament prophecy demonstrated in chapters 13 and 34 of Isaiah. There, we read vivid descriptions of divine judgment upon Babylon and Eden that actually came to pass in history. When the prophets described God's judgment, they said things like, "For the stars of the heavens and their constellations will not give their light; the sun will be dark at its rising, and the moon will not shed its light" (Isa. 13:10) and "All the host of heaven shall rot away, and the skies roll up like a scroll. All their host shall fall, as leaves fall from the vine, like leaves falling from the fig tree" (Isa. 34:4). Sounds very much like the language of Jesus, doesn't it?

The language of divine judgment is frequently communicated by way of metaphor and figures. Amos 5:20 reads, "Is not the day of the LORD darkness, and not light, and gloom with no brightness in it?"

Throughout the Old Testament, there are various prophetic warnings to Israel concerning God's judgment. The book of Ezekiel stands out as a primary example. Ezekiel contains some of the most bizarre portions of Scripture, such as the description in chapter 1 of the whirling *merkabah*, the wheel within the wheel. Many believe that this is a reference to the chariot throne of God that carries Him to various portions of the world to bring judgment. This kind of language was used between Elijah and Elisha in 2 Kings 2:12: "And Elisha saw it and he cried, 'My father, my father! The chariots of Israel and its horsemen!' And he saw him no more." When God removed His glory from Jerusalem in Ezekiel 10, the *shekinah* cloud was accompanied by the chariot of God's judgment. In Matthew 24, the same kind of language is used by Jesus as He warns His people of what is to come.

Jesus says in verse 30, "Then will appear in heaven the sign of the Son of Man." I don't know of any commentator on the gospel of Matthew who speaks with dogmatic certainty about the true nature of this sign. But there are some strange observations in the writings of the Jewish historian, Josephus, regarding certain signs that were observed between AD 60 and 70, one of which was a blazing comet that crossed the sky. Consider one extraordinary passage from his writings. It seems so strange that Josephus gives the impression that he was reluctant to record this event.

Besides these [signs in the heavens], a few days after the feast, on the one and twentieth day of the month, a certain prodigious and incredible phenomenon occurred or appeared: I suppose the account of it would seem to be a fable, were it not related by those that saw it, and were not the events that followed it of so considerable a nature as to deserve such signals; for, before sun-setting, chariots and troops of soldiers in their armor were seen running about among the clouds, and surrounding of cities.

Moreover, at that feast which we call Pentecost, as the priests were going by night into the inner [court of the temple,] as their custom was, to perform their sacred ministrations, the priest said that, in the first place, they felt a quaking, and heard a great noise, and after that they heard a sound as of a great multitude, saying, "Let us remove hence."

So, the priests and multitudes of other people testified to the same chariots that surrounded the city also appearing in the clouds with multitudes of heavenly soldiers.

We'd probably be justified in calling them angels. Then an audible voice was heard from heaven saying, "Let us remove hence." It's almost exactly the same phenomenon that took place when God left Jerusalem in Ezekiel's time (Ezek. 10).

It seems to me that the most natural reading of Matthew 24:29–35 would be that everything Jesus said would happen has already taken place in history. He was not referring to a yet-future fulfillment from our standpoint. He was referring to a judgment upon the nation of Israel that took place in AD 70.

Chapter
Five

THE DAY
AND THE HOUR

Imagine getting a call at four o'clock in the afternoon from a robber. He says to you, "In order to make things fair, I wanted to let you know that at eight o'clock tonight I'm going to break in to your house and rob you blind." If you took him seriously, what would you do? You'd have the whole police department waiting for the robber, and you'd probably arm yourself to protect your family and possessions. Jesus makes a similar point as He continues in the Olivet Discourse.

But concerning that day and hour no one knows, not even the angels of heaven, nor the Son, but the Father only. For as were the days of Noah, so will be the coming of the Son of Man. For as in those days before the flood they were eating and drinking, marrying and giving in marriage, until the day when Noah entered the ark, and they were unaware until the flood came and swept them all away, so will be the coming of the Son of Man. Then two men will be in the field; one will be taken and one left. Two women will be grinding at the mill; one will be taken and one left. Therefore, stay awake, for you do not know on what day your Lord is coming. But know this, that if the master of the house had known in what part of the night the thief was coming, he would have stayed awake and would not have let his house be broken into. Therefore you also must be ready, for the Son of Man is coming at an hour you do not expect. (Matt. 24:36–44)

The plot thickens as we arrive at this portion of the Olivet Discourse, and the difficulties in interpretation are not slowing down in the least. Jesus seems to be shifting His emphasis at this point in the text. Some commentators believe that until verse 35, Jesus had been simply speaking about the destruction of Jerusalem. But at this point in the text, He shifts His attention to matters concerning His ultimate coming at the time of the consummation of His kingdom. Others argue that even the previous passages that refer to His coming in glory did not refer to His coming in AD 70, but rather to His final, climactic coming at the end of history. Still others maintain that Jesus is following a prophetic pattern from the Old Testament.

Oftentimes with Old Testament prophecy there would be a near fulfillment, but also an ultimate fulfillment in the future. This particular passage has also been seen as a rebuttal to my position that these matters have already taken place in the past.

It is important to remember that this whole discourse was provoked by Jesus' announcement that the temple would be destroyed in Jerusalem. In light of this announcement, the disciples asked Him two questions. First, "When will these things take place?" and second, "What will be the sign of your coming and of the end of the age?"

It would be much easier if Jesus had answered the first

question with the signs that He gives—famines, earthquakes, and wars—and then finished by saying, "This generation will not pass away until all these things take place" (v. 34), and only then went on to speak about His coming. Unfortunately for the task of interpretation, He says, "all these things." Most would believe that "all these things" would refer to all three events—the destruction of the temple, the destruction of Jerusalem, and Christ's coming. This is the issue that has provoked so much skepticism and criticism of both Jesus and the trustworthiness of the Bible.

I'm amazed by this skepticism. My understanding of Jesus' words is that He is essentially saying, "I can tell you these things are all going to take place within the next forty years but I don't know what year, month, day, or hour." In chapter one, I used the illustration of predicting the demise of the United States within twelve months but not knowing the specific day or hour in no way negates the veracity of the prediction. Therefore, the first thing we see in this text is that Jesus does not retreat from His first prediction about the fulfillment of the things He prophesied.

In addition, many readers are bothered when Jesus says He doesn't know the day or the hour. If that is the case, how could He know that it would be within forty years? It would require supernatural knowledge to be able to predict the destruction of the temple and of Jerusalem with such astonishing accuracy. Why would His supernatural abilities be limited to generalities? Why can't Jesus give us more specific details?

This isn't much of a problem if we have an orthodox understanding of the incarnation. The Council of Chalcedon in AD 451 clearly acknowledged the mysterious nature of the incarnation, confessing Christ as having two natures—divine and human—in one person. Human beings are incapable of an exhaustive understanding of how the two natures of Jesus are united in one person. But Chalcedon did clearly define the boundaries of our speculation concerning the mystery of the incarnation. The council stated that Jesus is *vera homo, vera deus,* meaning "truly man and truly God." His true humanity is united with the true deity of the second person of the Godhead. The boundary that the council established is seen in the Chalcedonian Creed's insistence that this union was without *mixture, confusion, separation,* or *division.* Each nature retained its own attributes. This means that the incarnation did not result in a single, mixed nature where the deity and the humanity are blended together such that the divine is not truly divine and the human is not truly human, resulting in a *tertium quid*—"a third thing" that is neither God nor man but something else. The council was very careful to insist that each nature of Jesus retains its own attributes. A deified human nature is no longer human and a humanized divine nature is no longer divine. But in the incarnation, the attributes of deity remain in the divine nature and the attributes of humanity remain in the human nature.

There are times in Jesus' earthly ministry when He clearly manifests His human nature. For example, He was hungry, tired, and susceptible to physical pain. Since Jesus was a true human being, His human nature did not possess omniscience. On the other hand, the divine nature frequently communicated supernatural knowledge to the human nature of Jesus. There were times that Jesus spoke things that no human being could ever know. But this truth doesn't mean the divine nature communicated everything to the human nature. So when Jesus says, "I don't know the day and the hour," he's speaking of His humanity. The human nature is not omniscient. According to His humanity, Jesus knew that the time frame for His prophecies would be within forty years, but not the rest of the details. We create many problems for ourselves when we attempt to deify the human nature of Jesus. In this case, Jesus' human nature knew the general time frame of the generation, but not the day and the hour.

He goes on to describe the circumstances of His coming. I'm not sure if He is simply speaking of the judgment of Jerusalem or also about what will happen at the time of His final appearance, but in either case, there is a sense of warning and urgency. He says in verse 37, "For as were the days of Noah, so will be the coming of the Son of Man." What do Noah and Jesus have in common here?

God told Noah of the coming rain and commanded Noah to get to work building an ark. Can you imagine how his friends must have ridiculed him? But Noah just kept hammering away while the people kept laughing, giving no heed to the judgment that was coming. In the days of Noah, people would have been eating and drinking, marrying and being given in marriage, until the day that Noah entered the ark and it started to rain. All the scoffers found out soon enough that Noah knew exactly what he was doing.

Today, the whole world is filled with people who scoff like Noah's critics. Our Lord warns that each of us will be called to account, but no one knows when this will take place. But we're at ease, eating and drinking, and we make fun of those who warn of the judgment of God. Isn't God a God of love, after all? As it was in the days of Noah, so shall it be in the coming of the Son of Man. God's judgment will fall when no one is looking for it or expecting it.

Jesus says in verses 43 and 44, "But know this, that if the master of the house had known in what part of the night the thief was coming, he would have stayed awake and would not have let his house be broken into. Therefore you also must be ready, for the Son of Man is coming at an hour you do not expect."

Many have tried to predict the hour for Jesus' return, but every last one has been wrong. Jesus does not give us a calendar, but says, "Be ready. Watch." In another place, He ends by asking, "When the Son of Man comes, will he find faith on earth?" (Luke 18:8). Jesus is referring to His final return. If He comes before I die, I want to make sure He finds faith in me. Whether He comes now or whether you go to Him at your death, there will be a reckoning and judgment that no human can escape. We need to be ready. We need to be prepared. We need to be vigilant.

THE FAITHFUL AND WICKED SERVANTS

Imagine that you went out to dinner and ordered your meal, and the server said to you, "That's a fine selection. Unfortunately, we are running a little bit behind in the kitchen right now, but if you'll be patient, we'll have your dinner prepared to your liking sometime within the next three hours." I don't think you would be too happy with that. No one likes to wait forever for their food when they go out to eat. We are accustomed to waiting ten to twenty minutes for a meal, but if our wait time approaches an hour or so, even at a nice restaurant, we might ask the manager if there is a problem. If we are left waiting for our food any longer than that, we'd know for certain that something was wrong. Someone is not doing his job.

The concept of doing one's duty is an important theme as we continue to examine the Olivet Discourse. As He concludes the discourse, Jesus speaks of the faithful servant, who executes his duties well and in a timely fashion, and the wicked servant, who does not. Jesus has been warning His disciples to diligently to watch for His return. Let's consider the rest of the chapter.

> Who then is the faithful and wise servant, whom his master has set over his household, to give them their food at the proper time? Blessed is that servant whom his master will find so doing when he comes. Truly, I say to you, he will set him over all his possessions. But if that wicked servant says to himself, "My master is delayed," and begins to beat his fellow servants and eats and drinks with drunkards, the master of that servant will come on a day when he does not expect him and at an hour

he does not know and will cut him in pieces and put him with the hypocrites. In that place there will be weeping and gnashing of teeth. (Matt. 24:45–51)

When I was in seminary, one of the professors was Dr. Markus Barth, son of the famous Swiss theologian Karl Barth. I remember being astonished when Markus Barth produced a two-hundred-page academic paper on the first few words of Paul's letter to the Romans: "Paul, a slave of Jesus Christ." Many weighty tomes have been written about the words *Jesus Christ*, but what amazed me was that the whole focus of Barth's manuscript was on the single word *slave*.

The word that Jesus uses that is translated as "servant" is sometimes translated as "slave." People have a negative reaction to that word, but the great irony of the New Testament teaching is that no one ever becomes truly free until they become a slave of Jesus Christ. All of us are slaves of one sort or another. We're either slaves of Christ or slaves of sin. There's no other option for humanity.

One of Paul's favorite metaphors for the Christian's status in Christ is, "You are not your own" (1 Cor. 6:19). What does he mean by that? Paul's point is that Christians can never consider themselves autonomous. He goes on to explain that we are not our own because we've been bought with a price (v. 20). Jesus paid the asking price of our salvation. Paul's metaphor is vital to the Christian life.

Jesus asks, "Who then is the faithful and wise servant?" This is a question of fidelity. Who is a faithful servant? It's a strange term to use regarding a servant who is under the complete ownership of another. But the simplest meaning of a faithful servant is one who is full of faith, who can be trusted, and who is consistent in allegiance to his owner.

Jesus goes on to say in verse 45, "Who then is the faithful and wise servant, whom his master has set over his household, to give them their food at the proper time?" The master went on a journey and called one of his servants to be the steward of the house while he is away. This master put his servant in charge of all of the affairs of the house. We notice that Jesus emphasizes that timeliness is important. Jesus spoke of the faithful servant who was responsible not only to provide the food, but also to provide it on time. He said that this servant would be blessed if the master found him doing his job when he returned. The good servant, the faithful and wise servant, is the one who does what his master calls him to do. Jesus says in verse 47, "Truly, I say to you, he will set him over all his possessions." The master will give the servant even more responsibility and esteem because he has been faithful in the things given to him. This echoes Jesus' words in Luke 16:10 that he who wants to be given more responsibility in the kingdom must first be faithful in little things.

Jesus then describes the wicked servant in verses 48–51: "But if that wicked servant says to himself, 'My master is delayed,' and begins to beat his fellow servants and eats and drinks with drunkards, the master of that servant will come on a day when he does not expect him and at an hour he does not know and will cut him in pieces and put him with the hypocrites. In that place there will be weeping and gnashing of teeth." Here the wicked servant is having an internal dialogue. He thinks, "My master's gone. Who knows when he's coming back? Who knows if he's ever coming back? It's time to party! My master is delayed and I can do what I want."

You may not relate to the wicked servant entirely, but most of us have jobs and employers. How do you work when no one is looking? Are you on task? Are you committed to the responsibility that has been given to you? Or, when there is no supervisor to watch you, do you take advantage of the gap in oversight and do whatever you want?

Why is it that our behavior changes when no one is watching? Why do businesses have clocks where workers have to punch in every day? Why can't we just expect people to come to work and leave when they're supposed to? It's because of sin. It's because we have a tendency to behave in one way when we are being watched and act differently when we're free of supervision. Consider the parable of the prodigal son in Luke 15:11–32. Isn't it interesting that the son took his father's inheritance to a far-off country to squander it? He did this because nobody knew him in the foreign land. Nobody was watching. He could be free from all restraint.

The wicked servant is neither faithful nor wise. He is like the fool in Psalm 53:1 who says in his heart, "There is no God." The most serious and fatal self-delusion of the wicked is their belief that God will not judge them. The Bible tells us that God is long-suffering and patient. The reason for this kindness and mercy is to give us time to repent and turn to Christ. But we should never assume that God's gracious patience means that He won't call us to account. Many are tempted to think this way. In this passage, Jesus is addressing those who assume that the Master will never return. They think this gives them license to do whatever they want. No supervision. No faithfulness. No trust. No wisdom.

The master of the servant will come on a day when the servant isn't looking for him, and at an hour of which he is unaware. And the master will say to the faithful servant, "I left you with responsibility. I blessed you. I gave you an elevated status in my kingdom and increased responsibility." But to the wicked slave there will be nothing but judgment and separation from the house of the master. The response of the wicked slave will be weeping and gnashing of teeth.

Have you ever seen a person weep and gnash their teeth? I once knew a man who was caught in a very serious sin. He began to cry, wail, and sob. Nothing could comfort him. As his weeping was drawing to an end he said, "How could I have done this? Why did I do this?" This is going to be the scene of those who have ignored their master.

So the obvious question is, What will you be doing when He comes? Will He find you faithful? Not casually or occasionally, but all the time? Christ has bought us for Himself, and He has given us a task to perform whether we can physically see Him or not. May He find us faithful when He comes.

Further your Bible study with *Tabletalk* magazine, another learning tool from R.C. Sproul.

....

TABLETALK MAGAZINE FEATURES:

- A Bible study for each day—bringing the best in biblical scholarship together with down-to-earth writing, *Tabletalk* helps you understand the Bible and apply it to daily living.

- Trusted theological resource—*Tabletalk* avoids trends, shallow doctrine and popular movements to present biblical truth simply and clearly.

- Thought-provoking topics—each issue contains challenging, stimulating articles on a wide variety of topics related to theology and Christian living.

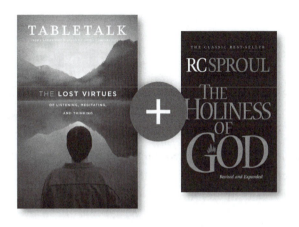

Sign up for a free 3-month trial of *Tabletalk* magazine and we will send you R.C. Sproul's *The Holiness of God*

TryTabletalk.com/CQ

About the Author

Dr. R.C. Sproul is the founder and chairman of Ligonier Ministries, an international multimedia ministry based in Sanford, Florida. He also serves as co-pastor at Saint Andrew's, a Reformed congregation in Sanford, and as chancellor of Reformation Bible College, and his teaching can be heard around the world on the daily radio program *Renewing Your Mind*.

During his distinguished academic career, Dr. Sproul helped train men for the ministry as a professor at several theological seminaries.

He is the author of more than ninety books, including *The Holiness of God*, *Chosen by God*, *The Invisible Hand*, *Faith Alone*, *Everyone's a Theologian*, *Truths We Confess*, *The Truth of the Cross*, and *The Prayer of the Lord*. He also served as general editor of *The Reformation Study Bible* and has written several children's books, including *The Donkey Who Carried a King*.

Dr. Sproul and his wife, Vesta, make their home in Longwood, Florida.